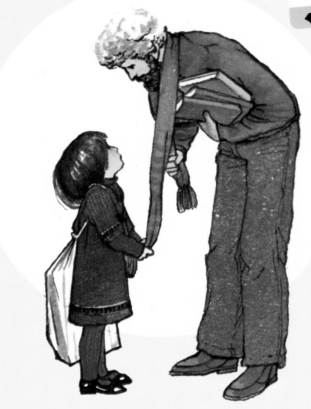

For Paul

KESTREL BOOKS
Published by Penguin Books Ltd
Harmondsworth, Middlesex, England

Copyright © 1981 by Jan Ormerod

First published in 1981

ISBN 0 7226 5736 6
Printed in Great Britain

Jan Ormerod

Sunshine

Kestrel Books

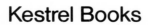

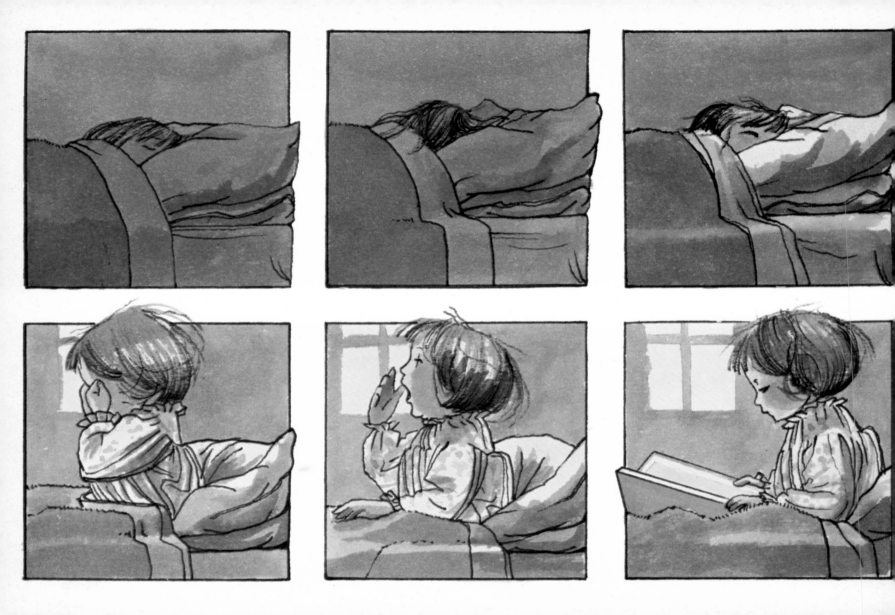

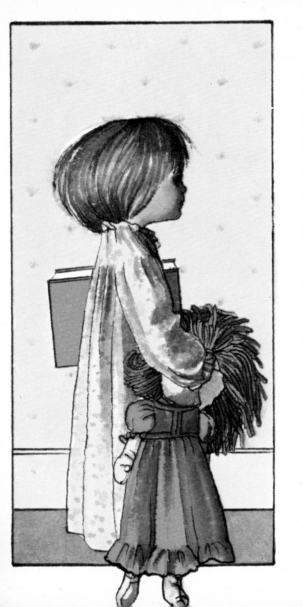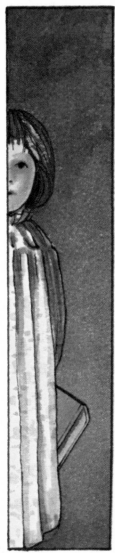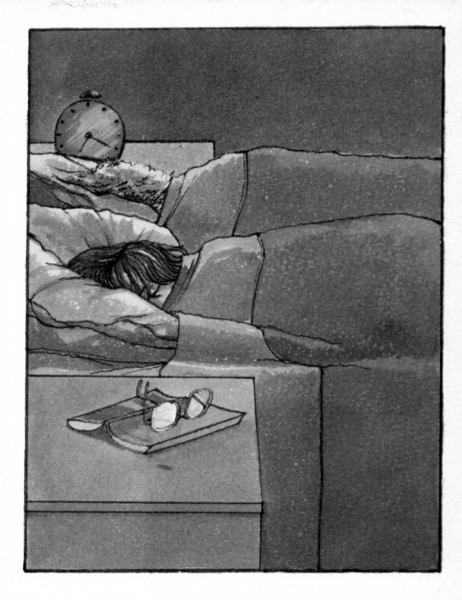

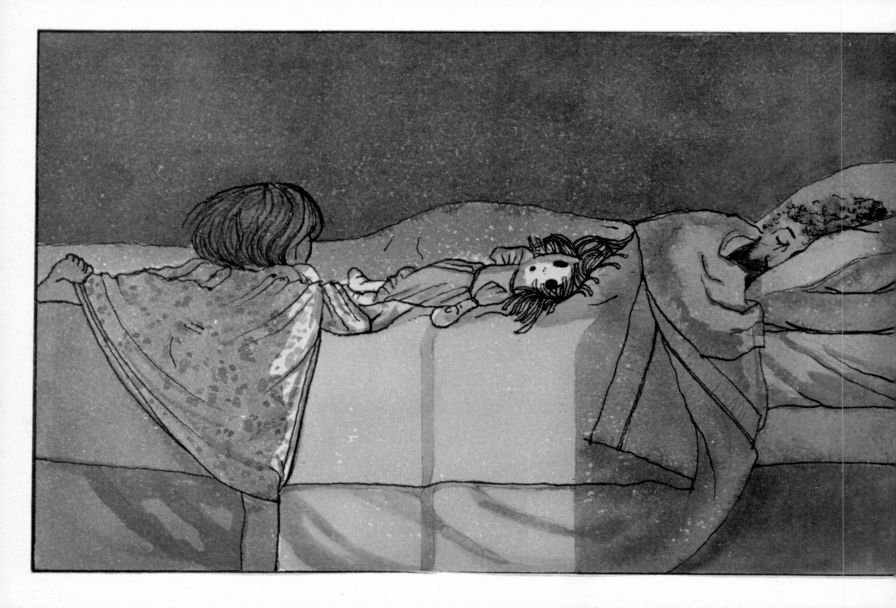

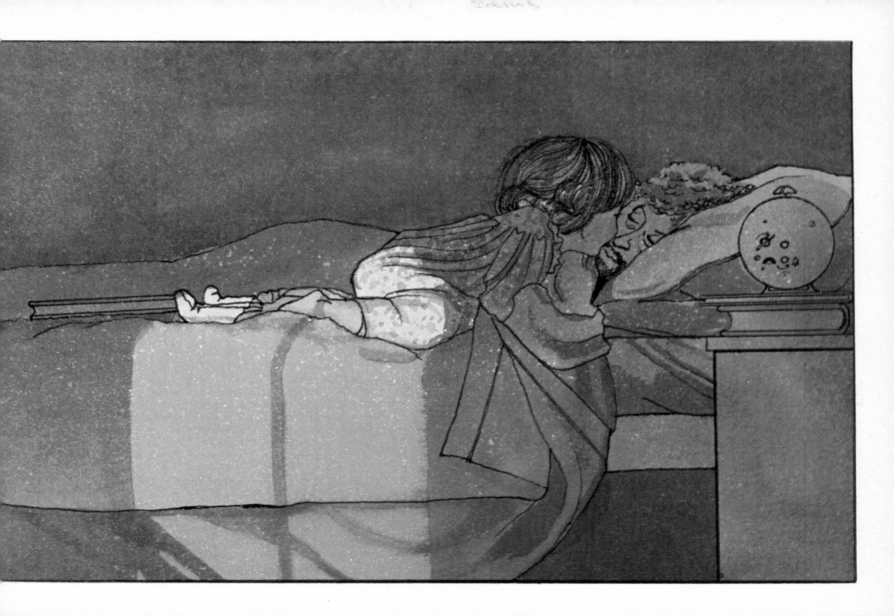

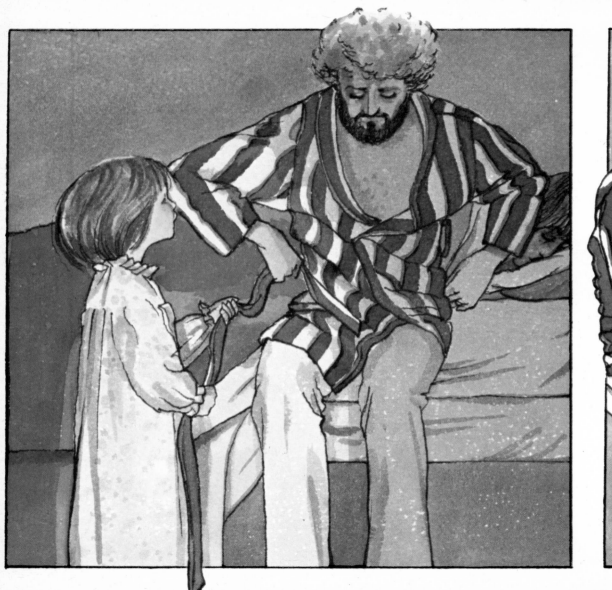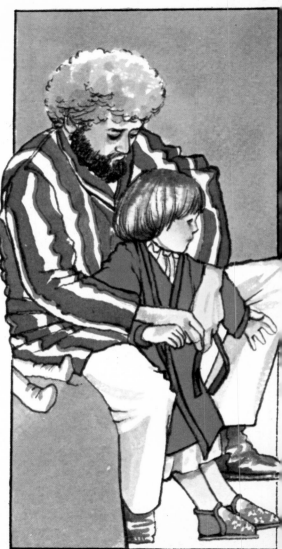

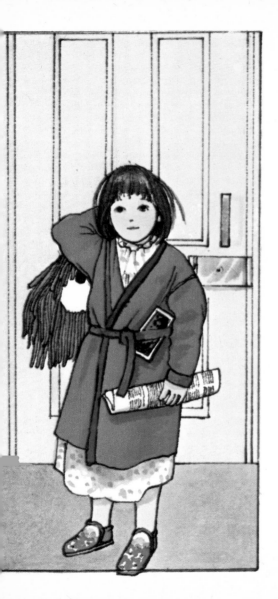
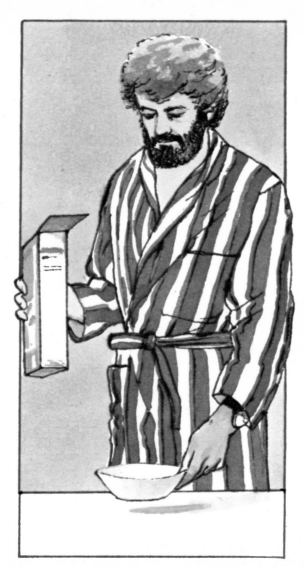
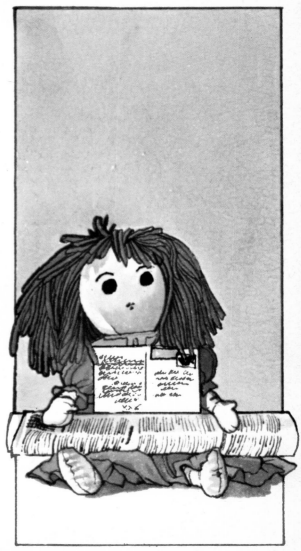

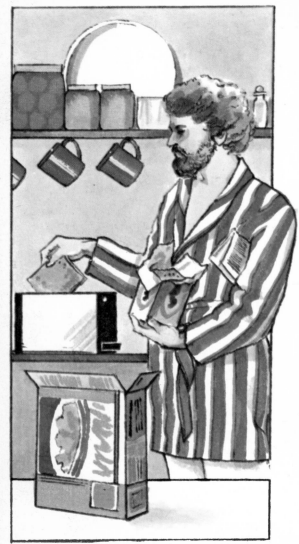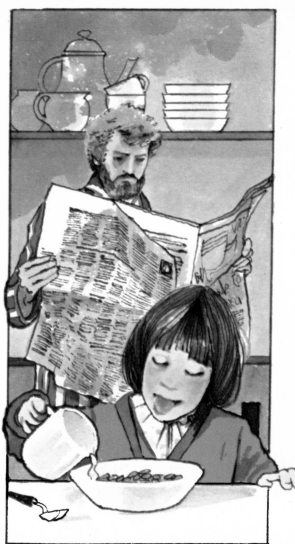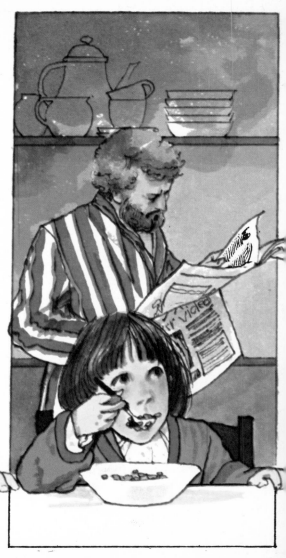

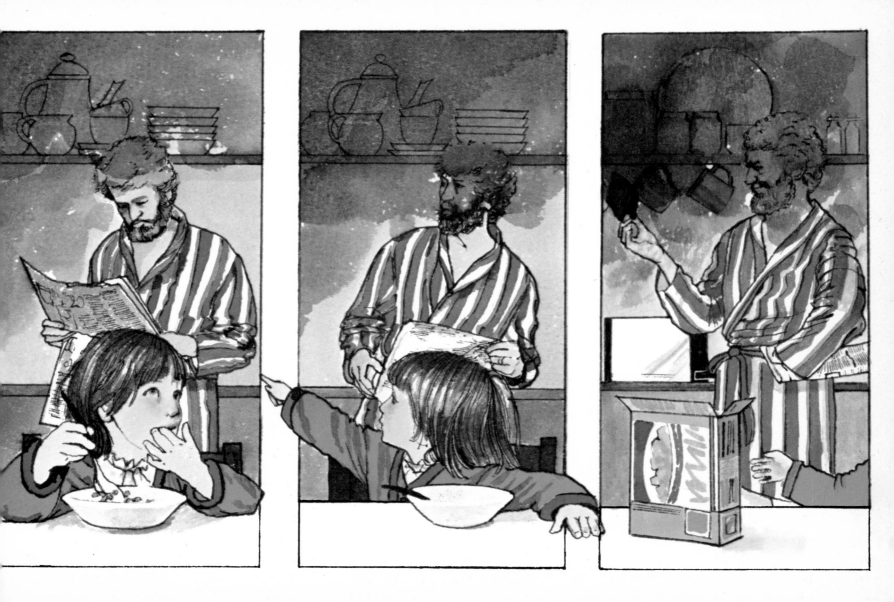

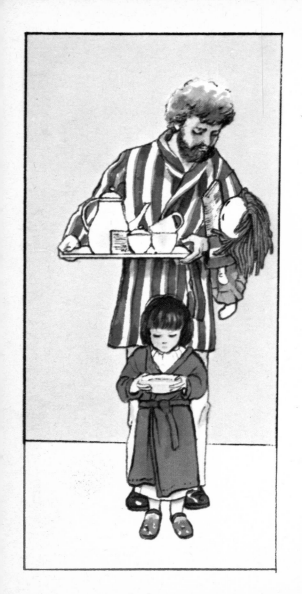
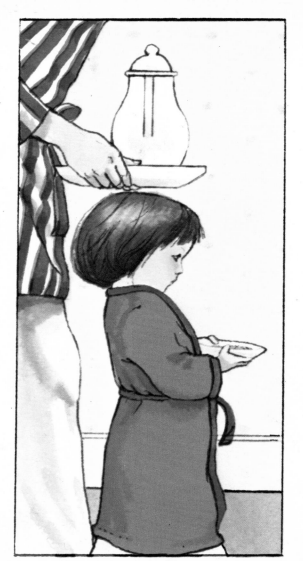
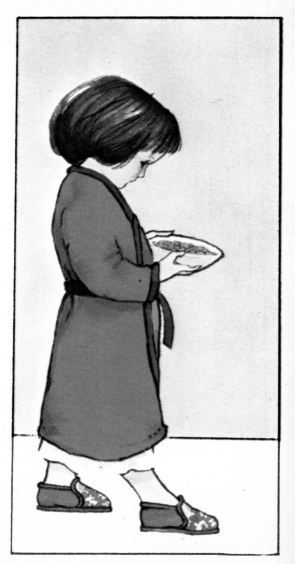

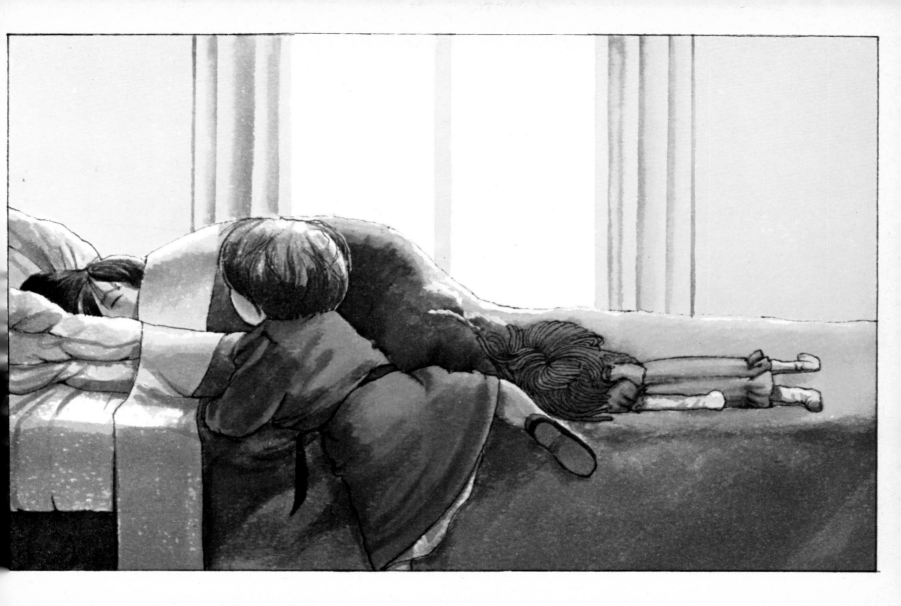

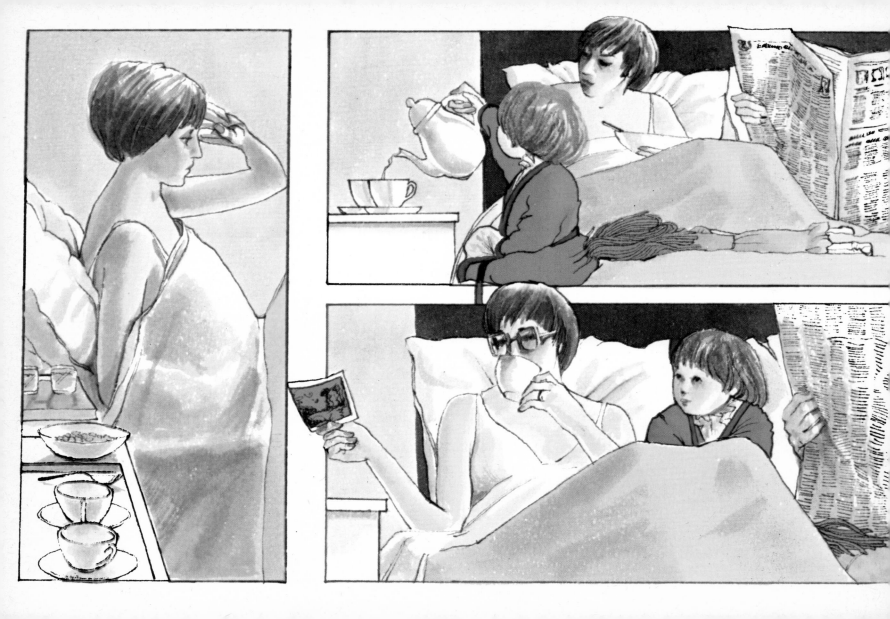

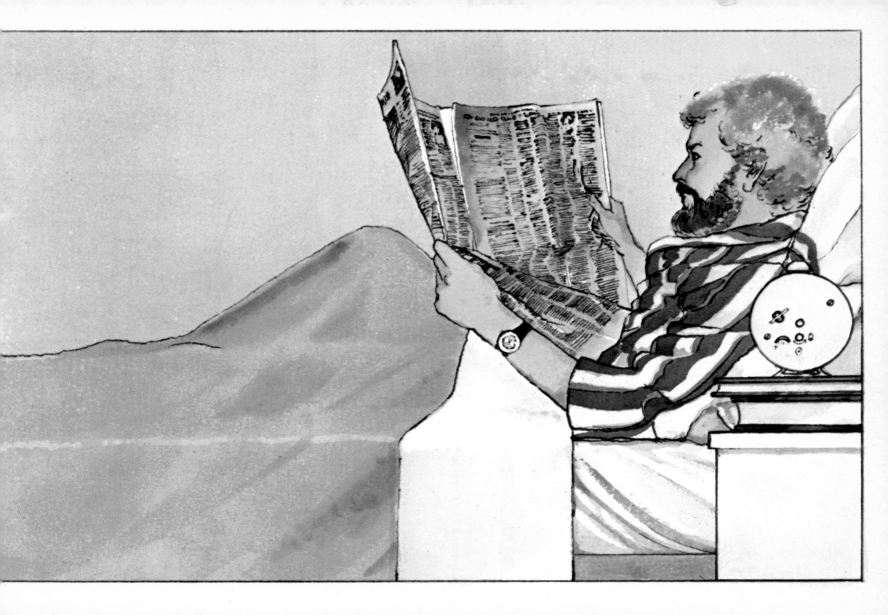

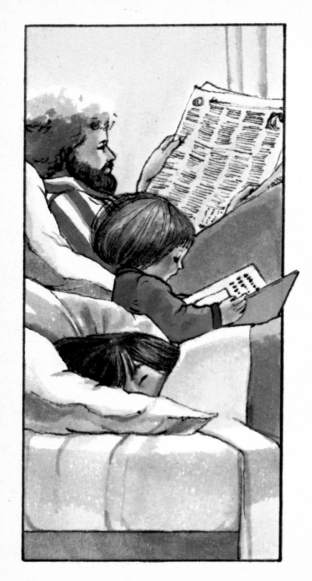
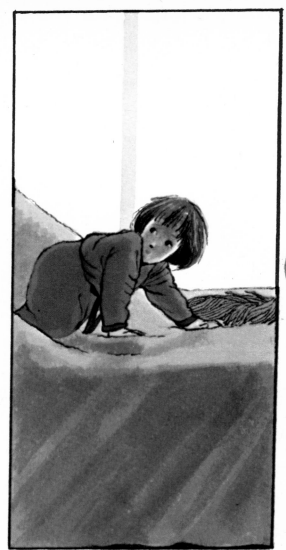
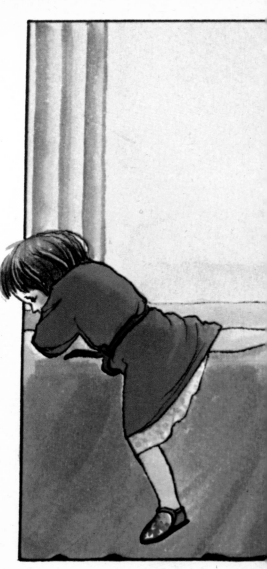

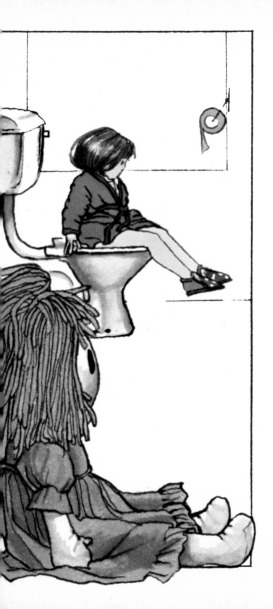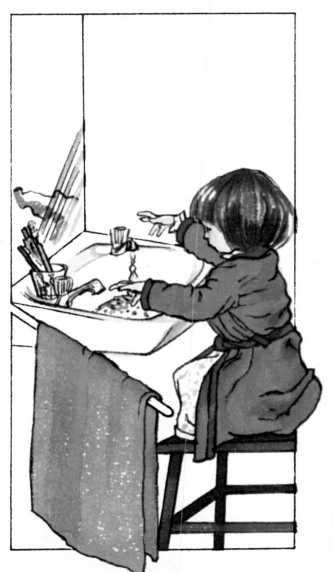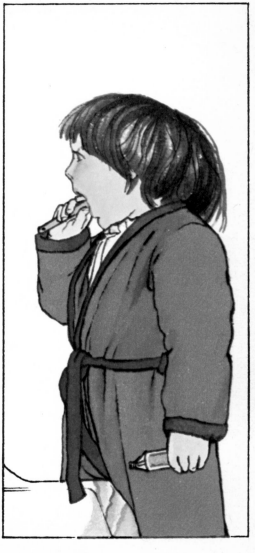

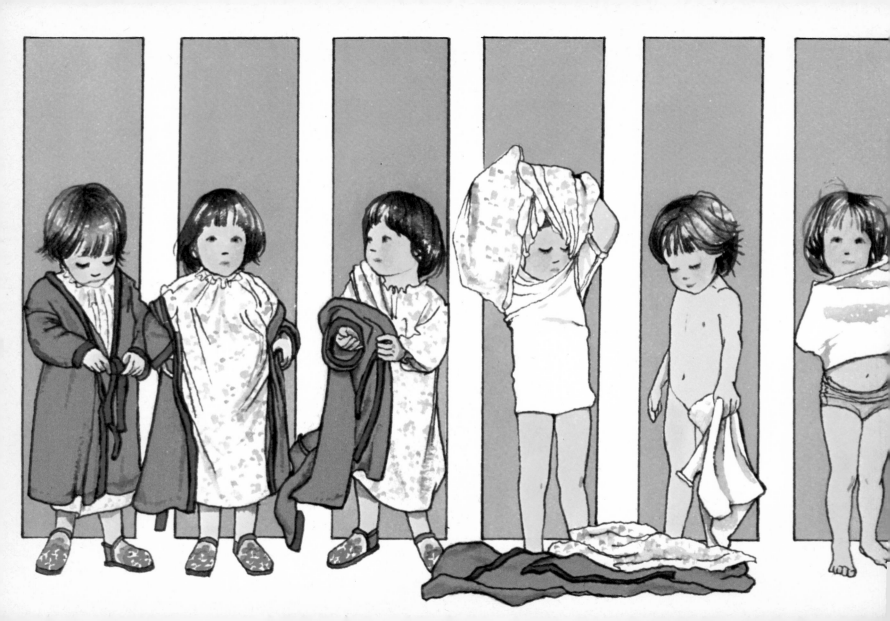

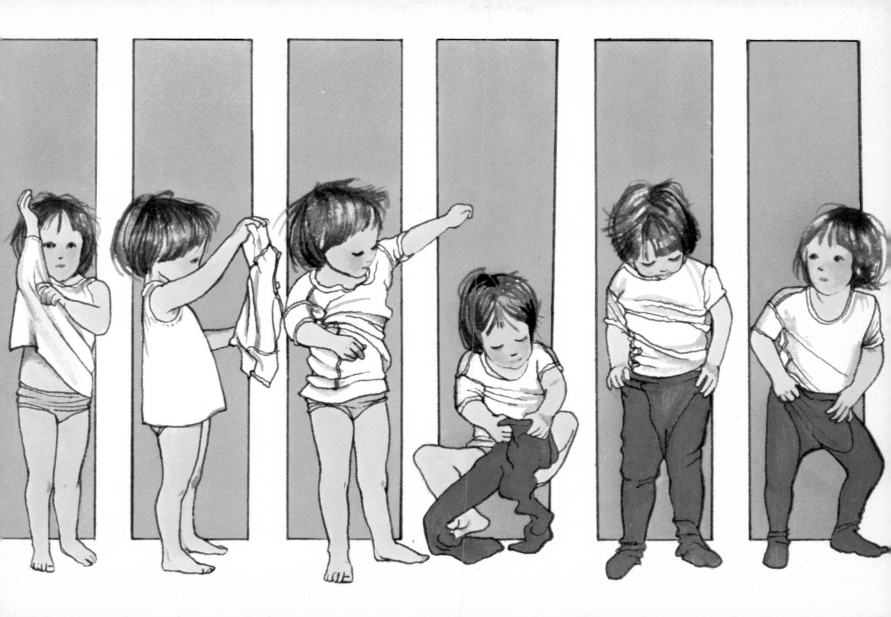

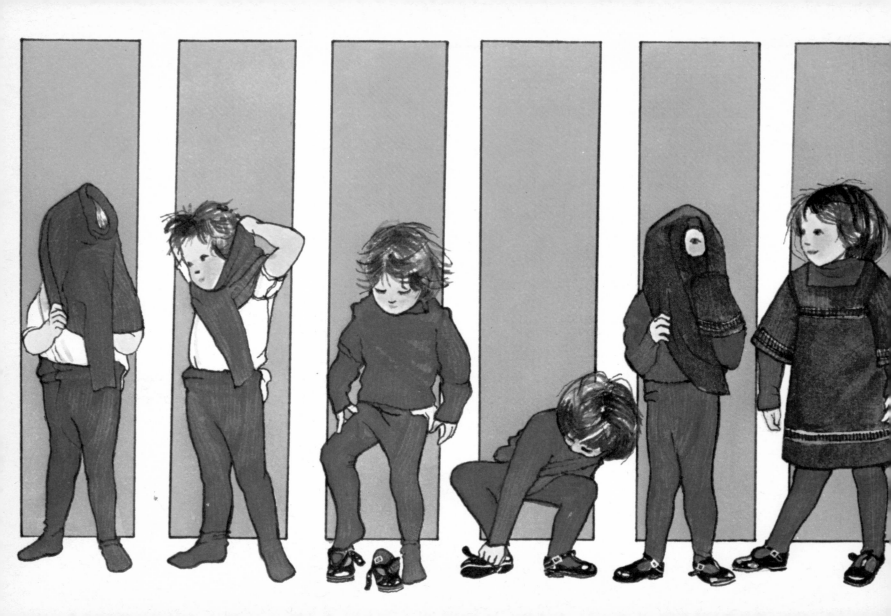

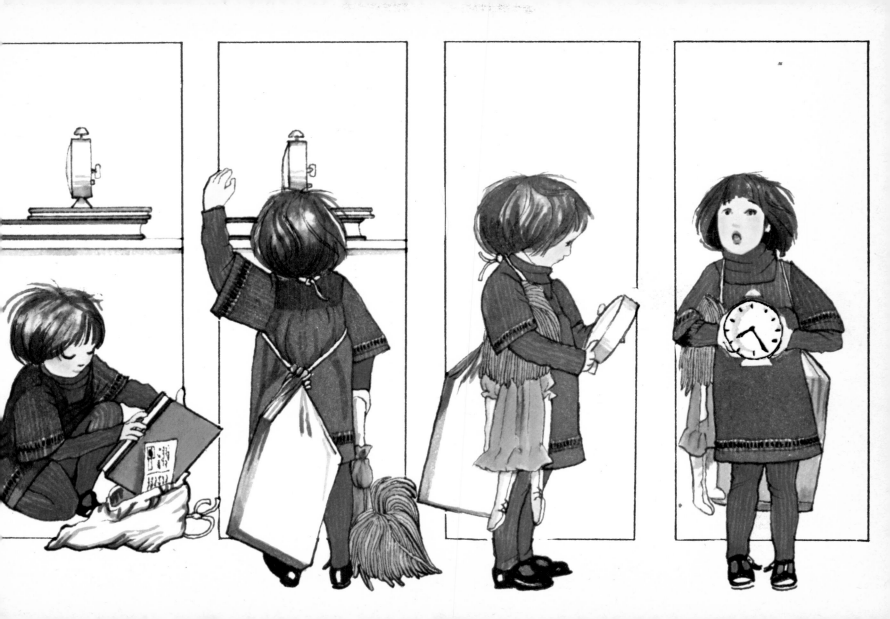

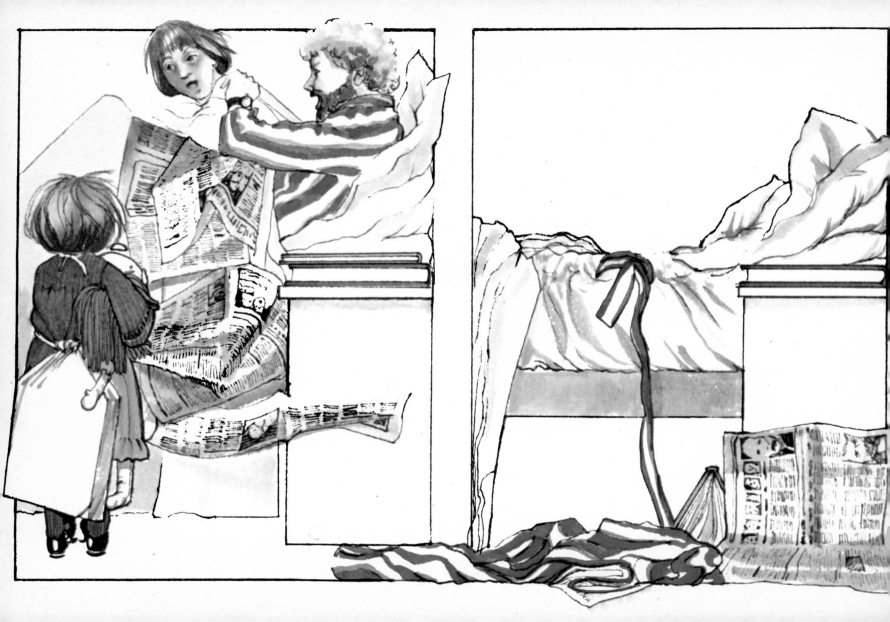

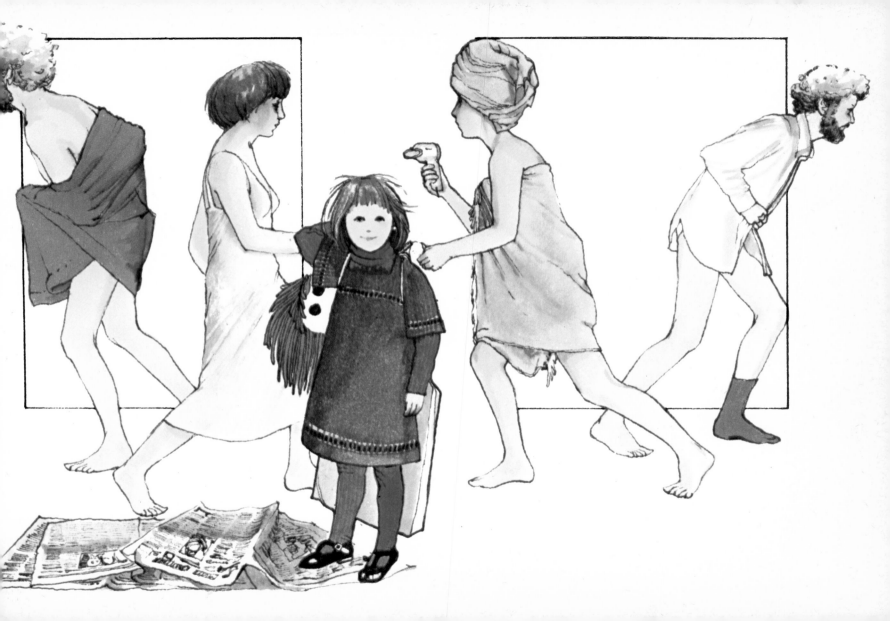

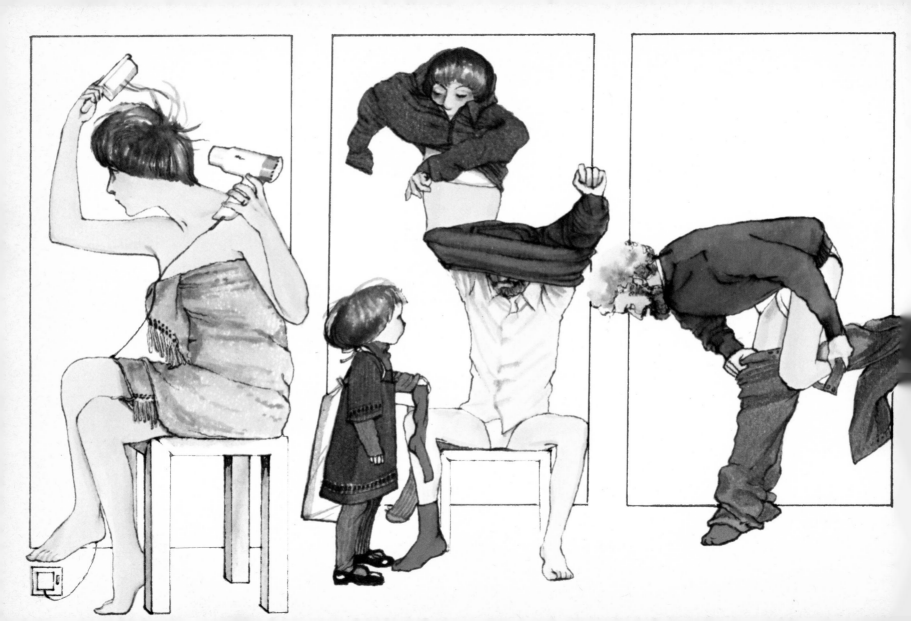

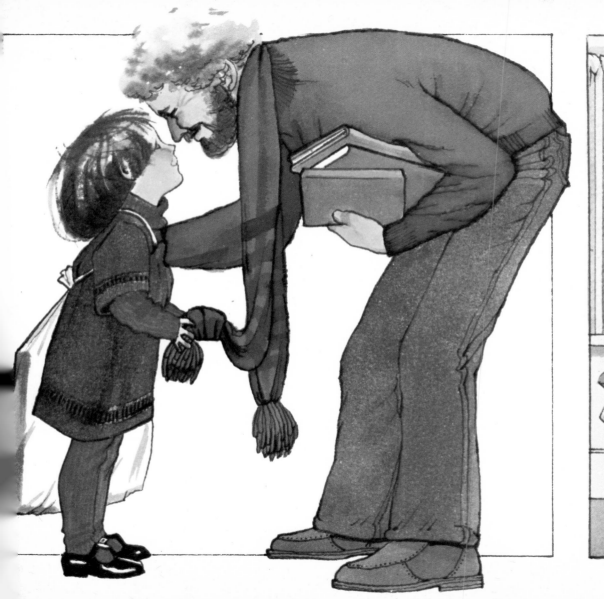
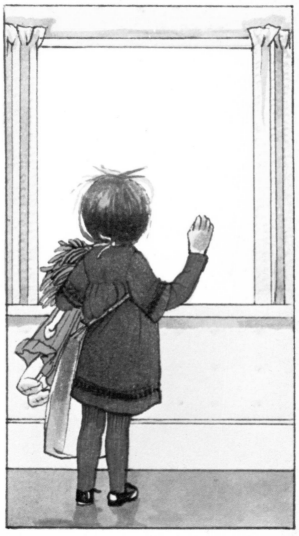

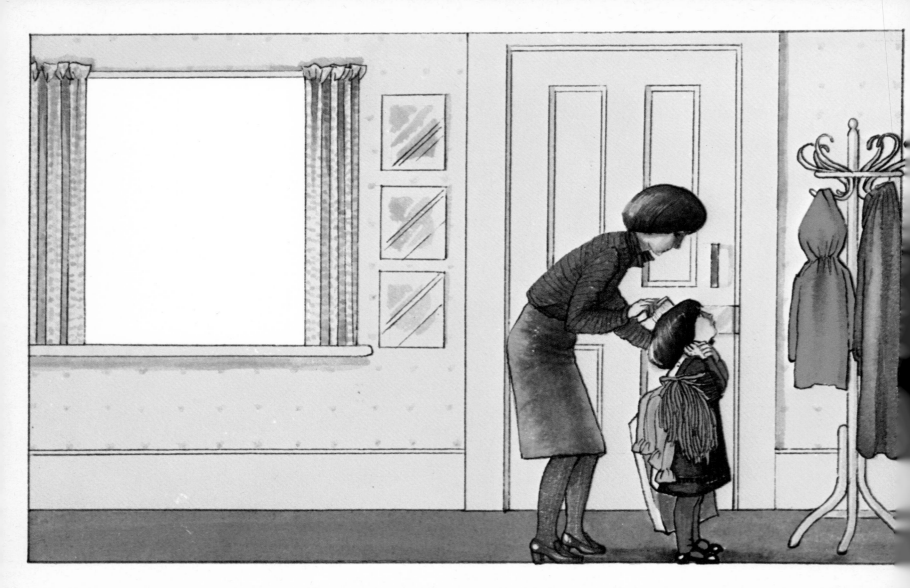

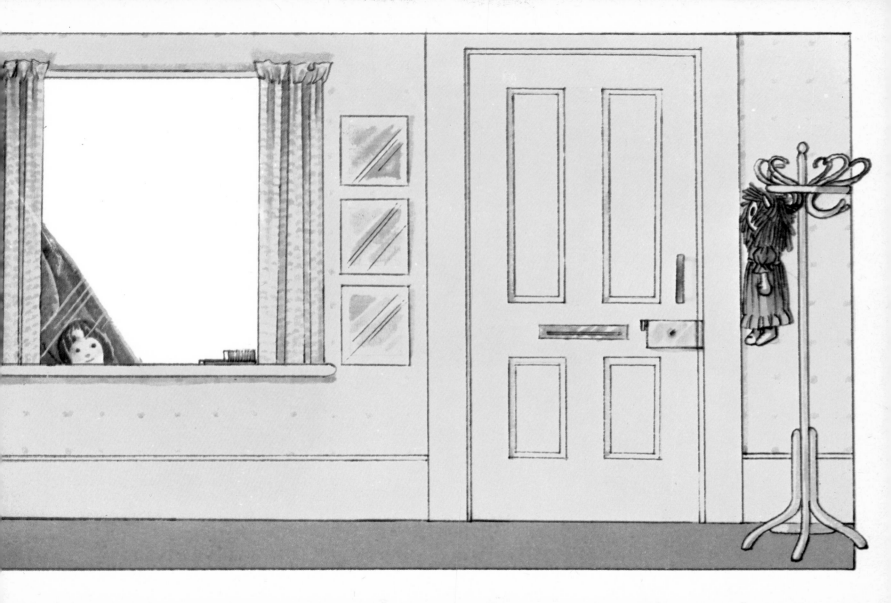

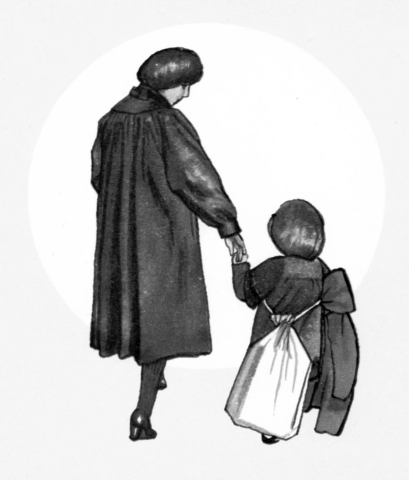